Original title:
Echoes of Magic

Copyright © 2024 Creative Arts Management OÜ
All rights reserved.

Author: Gideon Barrett
ISBN HARDBACK: 978-9916-90-084-0
ISBN PAPERBACK: 978-9916-90-085-7

The Silent Language of the Universe

In shadows deep, stars softly glow,
Whispers of night, secrets to show.
Galaxies dance in a cosmic waltz,
Time stands still, no reason, no faults.

Words unspoken, within starlit dreams,
Silent echoes flow in moonbeams.
Thoughts intertwined like celestial streams,
A boundless canvas with infinite themes.

A Tapestry of Celestial Whispers

Threads of light weave through the dark,
Each twinkle a tale, a memory spark.
Nebulas flourish in color so bright,
Cradled softly in the arms of the night.

Galactic motifs swirl through the air,
Boundless horizons, a vision rare.
Celestial whispers wrap 'round my soul,
Woven together, they make me whole.

Lighthouses of Lost Enchantments

On distant shores, where dreams collide,
Lighthouses shine, a beacon, our guide.
Lost in the mist, stories unfold,
Whispers of magic in echoes of old.

Through tempest and calm, they stand so tall,
A sanctuary for hearts that call.
In twilight's embrace, we wander near,
Seeking the warmth of forgotten cheer.

Elysian Thoughts of Twilight

As day surrenders to dusky hues,
Elysian dreams come softly like dew.
Fading light drapes the world in gold,
A tender lullaby, gentle and bold.

In tranquil moments, our spirits unite,
Floating on whispers that fill the night.
Twilight unveils the magic it keeps,
In the stillness, the universe sleeps.

Elixirs of the Moonlit Night

In shadows deep, the whispers flow,
Alchemy of dreams begins to glow.
Stars above like lanterns bright,
Crafting secrets in the night.

Potions brewed with silver light,
Each drop sings of pure delight.
Mystic herbs and ancient lore,
Awaken hearts, forevermore.

Songs from the Enchanted Forest

Whispers dance through branches tall,
Nature's chorus, a magic call.
Leaves and petals sing along,
Echoes of the earth's sweet song.

Creatures stir in moonlit glades,
Unseen hands weave gentle shades.
Harmony in every breeze,
Melodies that flow with ease.

Chants of the Silver River

Ripples shimmer, stories told,
In the current, dreams unfold.
Moonlight paints a silver trail,
Rivers weave a timeless tale.

Voices rise where waters meet,
Softly singing, pure and sweet.
Nature's heart in rhythmic flow,
Guiding souls where spirits go.

Veils of Secret Sorcery

Behind the veil, shadows twine,
Magic brews in every line.
Spells are woven, soft and light,
Mysteries held in the night.

Cloaked in whispers, secrets swirl,
In the darkness, wonders twirl.
Enchantment lingers, soft and low,
Where the seeds of magic grow.

Twilight's Grimoire of Dreams

In twilight's hush, the shadows play,
Whispers of magic, night and day.
Stars adorn the velvet sky,
Where secrets of the heart can fly.

A book of spells upon my knee,
Each page an echo, a mystery.
Dreams woven in a silver seam,
A tapestry of hopes, a fleeting dream.

Hidden Pathways of Sorcery

Through ancient woods, the pathways wind,
Beneath the boughs, lost tales you'll find.
With each step, the air grows thick,
Mystic scents of candle wick.

Runes inscribed on stones so old,
Guarding secrets, stories told.
Whispers call from shadows cast,
In hidden realms, the die is cast.

Reflections in the Mystic Waters

Beneath the moon, the waters shine,
Mirrors of truth in sylvan twine.
Rippling dreams of worlds unseen,
Where every glance reveals the keen.

I see my face, but not my form,
In depths where magic does transform.
Each rippling wave a tale unfolds,
Of ages past and futures bold.

The Spellbinder's Heart

In every pulse, an ancient spell,
A heartbeat's hymn, a whispered bell.
With every tear, a potion brewed,
The alchemy of love pursued.

A binding force, both fierce and kind,
In shadows deep, true light we find.
Her heart, a charm that none can break,
With every vow, a promise make.

The Enigma of Floating Thoughts

In the quiet of the night,
Whispers dance like fireflies,
Drifting through the silent air,
Carrying secrets untold.

Beneath the moon's watchful gaze,
Dreams meander like the stars,
Each one a fleeting shadow,
A puzzle yet to be solved.

Threads of memories entwined,
In the tapestry of our mind,
What was lost, what was gained,
The riddle remains unclear.

Floating gently on the breeze,
Thoughts escape like wayward birds,
In their flight, they weave stories,
An enigma waiting to form.

Mysteries Adrift in Time

Time flows like a river wide,
Carrying echoes of the past,
Moments drift like autumn leaves,
Each one a whisper of fate.

Ancient tales lie in wait,
Guarded by the sands of hours,
In their depths, a secret waits,
To be uncovered by the brave.

As sunsets paint the horizon,
Colors blur and fade away,
Mysteries lost in twilight,
Yet hope ignites the unknown.

In the shadows of the dawn,
Footsteps mark the paths we tread,
In the silence of the morn,
Truths await to be unveiled.

Portals of Luminous Discovery

In the heart of the forest green,
Where light breaks through the leaves,
Portals shimmer in the sun,
Awakening dormant dreams.

Each step a chance to wander,
Into realms unseen by few,
Where knowledge blooms like flowers,
Colors vivid, ever new.

Voices echo on the breeze,
Carrying wisdom from afar,
In the embrace of twilight's glow,
Learning dances with the stars.

In this journey of the mind,
Discovery becomes our guide,
Through the gates of the unknown,
We find the light inside.

Lighthouses in the Night Sky

High upon the cliffs they stand,
Guardians of the ocean's edge,
Casting beams of silver light,
Guiding lost souls to the shore.

Stars twinkle like distant gems,
Illuminating the dark sea,
Each wave a silent story,
Of journeys long and journeys bold.

When the storm clouds gather fast,
And shadows threaten to engulf,
The lighthouses shine with hope,
A promise woven into night.

In their glow, we find our way,
Through the tempest and the calm,
Each beacon a reminder,
That light prevails over despair.

Incantations in the Stillness

In the hush of night's embrace,
Whispers swirl around with grace.
Silent shadows, secrets kept,
In the stillness, dreams are wept.

Moonlit paths of soft delight,
Guided by the stars so bright.
Voices echo in the dark,
Incantations, leaving marks.

Time, a river flowing slow,
Ancient tales begin to flow.
Breath of life in gentle sighs,
Awakens truths beneath the skies.

The Flickering Light of Reverie

In a corner where dreams ignite,
Flickers dance in soft twilight.
A moment caught, a fleeting glance,
Lost in the spell of a trance.

Whispers float on tender air,
Carrying stories laid bare.
With every pulse, a heart will race,
Chasing shadows in a space.

Memory's glow, a fleeting spark,
Guides the heart through the dark.
In the silence, thoughts align,
The light of reverie, divine.

Enigmas in the Mist

Veil of gray that shrouds the land,
Secrets woven, soft and grand.
Figures blurred in whispered dream,
In the mist, things aren't what they seem.

Echoes call from far away,
Luring minds that dare to stray.
Questions linger in the haze,
Lost in thought's perplexing maze.

Every droplet tells a tale,
Of forgotten paths, frail and pale.
Through the fog, we seek to find,
Enigmas whisper to the mind.

The Magic That Whispers

Beneath the leaves, a secret sigh,
Nature's pulse, a gentle cry.
In the breeze, enchanting tunes,
Songs of soft, ethereal moons.

The nightingale speaks in code,
Tales of love and dreams bestowed.
In the darkness, wishes bloom,
Magic stirs within the gloom.

Every glance, a brush of fate,
In this realm, we gravitate.
Whispers swirl like stars above,
Reminding us of endless love.

Mysterious Luminance of Dawn

In whispers soft, the shadows fade,
A golden glow begins to wade.
The night retreats, a gentle thief,
While dreams dissolve in dawn's motif.

The sky ignites, a canvas bright,
With hues that dance in morning light.
Each stroke a promise, rich and bold,
Of stories that the day will hold.

A tranquil hush, the world awakes,
With tender sighs, the silence breaks.
In dew-kissed grass, the hopes reside,
As nature breathes in joy and pride.

So let this day begin anew,
With mysteries that will ensue.
In every ray, a chance to find,
The magic woven in the mind.

The Harp of Fable's Echo

A melody, both sweet and rare,
Plays softly in the twilight air.
Each note a tale, a whispered thread,
Of dreams and wishes, long since said.

The strings of time, they shimmer bright,
As voices blend in softest light.
From ancient lands, the tales arise,
Beneath the gaze of soft, blue skies.

In every chord, a story lives,
Of loss and love, the heart forgives.
The harp sings on, its echoes weave,
A tapestry that we believe.

So gather 'round and lend an ear,
To fables old that still draw near.
For every song is bound to shine,
With truths that sparkle, pure and fine.

Flickers of Dreamlike Intrigue

A shadow flits, a subconscious dance,
In realms where hopes and fears advance.
With silken threads, the mind can weave,
Intriguing tales that hearts believe.

Through wisps of fog, the visions play,
A fleeting glimpse of night to day.
Each spark ignites a curious thought,
In webs of dreams, the soul is caught.

In corners dark, the secrets lie,
Beneath the watchful, starry sky.
Unlock the door, let visions stream,
And wander through the shrouded dream.

For every flicker, every sigh,
Hints at the truths we can't deny.
So chase the shadows, feel the thrill,
Of your own heart, the voice of will.

Essence of the Starborn

From cosmic depths, a whisper flows,
In stardust trails where magic grows.
The essence glows, a guiding light,
Through endless night, a wondrous sight.

Born from the heart of silent skies,
Each spark a dream that never dies.
With every breath, the universe sings,
Of timeless love and boundless wings.

In twilight's grasp, the cosmos hums,
As ancient rhythms beckon drums.
A tapestry of night unfurled,
An echo of the vast, wide world.

So stand beneath the starlit dome,
And let the night lead you back home.
For in this glow, the heart will find,
The essence of the starborn kind.

Manifestations of Starry Wonders

In the night sky, dreams unfold,
Stars whisper secrets, stories told.
Galaxies twinkle, worlds collide,
In the cosmic dance, we take pride.

Celestial lights, a shimmering brigade,
Every flicker, a wish conveyed.
Planets align in mystic embrace,
Echoes of magic time can't erase.

Nebulas swirl with colors bright,
Painting the canvas of endless night.
Constellations guide the wandering soul,
Mapping the journey toward the whole.

In the vastness where silence reigns,
The heart finds peace, and love gains.
Beneath the sky, we'll find our way,
Through manifestations of night and day.

Chasing Shadows in the Moonlight

Under the glow of silvery beams,
Shadows dance, weaving dreams.
Echoes of whispers, secrets to share,
In moonlit paths, we find the rare.

Figures linger, fleeting and bright,
Leading the way through the gentle night.
With every step, the shadows wane,
Yet they beckon, a playful chain.

Mysterious tales in the twilight breeze,
Floating softly among the trees.
Chasing echoes, we roam free,
While shadows uncover the hidden key.

In the silence, a heartbeat found,
Moonlight dances, enchantments abound.
We grasp the night, let worries go,
Chasing shadows, there's magic in the flow.

The Prelude to a Spellbinder's Tale

Once upon a time beneath a star,
A whisper arose from lands afar.
In shadows they gathered, cloaked in grace,
A spellbinder's play in a timeless space.

With wands aglow and hearts so light,
They conjured dreams that sparked the night.
Words of power, ancient and true,
Stirring the magic that flows anew.

Each incantation wove tales divine,
Threads of fate in a design.
As the moon hung low, a world awoke,
In every silence, a story spoke.

The winds whispered secrets, soft and low,
While stars aligned in a radiant show.
Gathering moments, let's not delay,
This is the prelude, the spellbinder's way.

Wandering Beyond the Veil of Reality

Beyond the veil where wonders blend,
Reality twists, time seems to bend.
Visions flicker, colors ignite,
In the realm of dreams, pure delight.

Through whispers of fate, we dare to roam,
In lands unknown, we find our home.
With every step, illusions fade,
In the tapestry of life, adventures made.

Glimmers of truth in a world surreal,
Echoes of love that we deeply feel.
As boundaries blur in twilight's embrace,
We wander freely, lost in grace.

In this dance of the mind and heart,
Every moment a work of art.
Beyond the veil, our spirits soar,
Wandering realms, forever explore.

Lullabies of the Enchanted Forest

In shadows deep where whispers play,
The ancient trees begin to sway.
Soft notes float through the evening air,
A melody of dreams laid bare.

Stars peek through the velvet night,
Guiding lost souls with their light.
Crickets sing their gentle tune,
Beneath the watchful gaze of moon.

The brook hums low, a soothing sound,
A cradle's rock upon the ground.
Fireflies dance in soft embrace,
Their flickers form a warming space.

So close your eyes, let worries cease,
Embrace the forest's tender peace.
For in this realm, both wild and free,
Lullabies weave your destiny.

Dancing Flames of Forgotten Spells

In the hearth where shadows dance,
Flames swirl in a molten trance.
Whispers of old begin to rise,
Casting secrets through the skies.

Embers glow with a golden hue,
Tales of magic come anew.
Flickering tongues of fiery grace,
Reveal the past we all must face.

Cinders crackle, soft and bright,
Illuminating the darkened night.
Each spark a wish, a hope, a dream,
In the flames, we find our theme.

Let the warmth embrace your heart,
In this dance, we all take part.
For forgotten spells weave and twirl,
Bringing magic to our world.

Murmurs from the Crystal Cavern

In the depths where silence reigns,
Crystal echoes break the chains.
Soft whispers of the earth arise,
A symphony of ancient sighs.

Stalactites drip with gentle grace,
Mirrored secrets find their place.
Glow of gems in shadows played,
Veils of mystery softly laid.

Rivers run beneath the stone,
Tales of ages long since flown.
Breathe in the chill, feel the air,
As whispers weave without a care.

In this cavern, time stands still,
Nature's pulse, it seeks to fill.
Embrace the murmurs, let them guide,
Through crystal halls, let magic bide.

Reverberations of Ancient Charms

In a grove where shadows dwell,
Ancient charms weave their spell.
Each leaf holds a whispered lore,
　　Echoes of a time once more.

The wind carries a timeless tune,
Reverberates with the light of moon.
Mystic chants in twilight's fold,
Stories from the brave and bold.

Branches sway with a knowing grace,
Guarding secrets in their embrace.
As night falls, the world stands still,
Ancient magic bends to will.

So linger here, let spirits roam,
Within this realm we call our home.
For in these echoes, life unfolds,
Reverberations of tales yet told.

The Marvels Beneath Whispering Trees

Beneath the boughs, secrets dwell,
Nature's whispers, stories to tell.
In the cool shade, dreams take flight,
Life dances softly, hidden from sight.

Roots entwined in earth's embrace,
Time moves gently, leaves interlace.
Each rustle sings of ancient lore,
Where magic blooms forevermore.

In twilight's glow, shadows play,
Silver beams guide the way.
Through fragrant paths, we wander free,
Unraveling wonders 'neath whispering trees.

Symphony of a Shimmering Horizon

Dawn awakens, colors ignite,
A canvas dressed in pure delight.
Waves of gold and hues of blue,
Nature's symphony, fresh and new.

The sun ascends, a fiery crown,
Painting the skies, lifting the frown.
Beyond the cliffs, where sea meets sky,
Whispers of dreams begin to fly.

Each heartbeat thunders, music alive,
In the brilliance where visions thrive.
Harmony dances, flowing like streams,
In the embrace of shimmering dreams.

Fragments of Myth in Modern Light

Stories woven, threads of old,
In every heart, a tale unfolds.
Legends whisper through city streets,
Echoes of gods in life's repeats.

Amidst the chaos, shadows stir,
Myths awaken, memories blur.
Faces of heroes, lost and found,
In each sunrise, their hopes resound.

Modern tales with ancient grace,
A dance of time, a timeless chase.
Fragments of truth, elusive and bright,
Illuminated now in modern light.

The Chronicle of Effervescent Realities

In a world spun with dreams untold,
Mirrors reflect the brave and bold.
Bubbles of laughter, moments so sweet,
Every heartbeat finds its beat.

Through paths of wonder, we boldly stride,
Chasing the glimmers that dance inside.
The fabric of existence sways and bends,
A tapestry where the story never ends.

With each turn, the vibrant spark,
Guides us onward, igniting the dark.
In this chronicle, we find our place,
Effervescent in time, filled with grace.

The Sorceress's Serenade

In shadows deep, her whispers flow,
Enchanting hearts with a gentle glow.
A melody woven from ancient lore,
The sorceress sings, forevermore.

With starlit grace, she casts her spell,
Each note a tale of magic to tell.
The night awakens, the spirits dance,
Lost in the rhythm, caught in a trance.

Her voice like silk, soft and warm,
Guiding the lost through storm and swarm.
In dreams she lingers, a fleeting shade,
The sorceress's serenade is played.

As dawn draws near, the echoes fade,
But in the heart, her song is laid.
A timeless ballad, ethereal, bold,
The magic of night will never grow old.

Ethereal Secrets in Twilight

Beneath the veil of twilight's embrace,
Lies a realm of secrets, a hidden place.
Whispers of ancients trail on the breeze,
In ethereal shadows, the mind finds ease.

The stars align in a cosmic dance,
Illuminating dreams with a fleeting glance.
In twilight's hush, realities blur,
Magic awakens with a silent stir.

Veils of the past in the night unfold,
Ethereal stories waiting to be told.
Each secret murmured, a fragile sigh,
In the heart of twilight, spirits fly.

Awash in colors of purple and gold,
Life's hidden wonders begin to unfold.
In the stillness, we find our way,
Ethereal secrets, forever to stay.

Fables of the Hidden Realm

In forests thick where shadows blend,
Whispers of fables from ages send.
Creatures lurking 'neath the ancient trees,
Guardians of tales carried by the breeze.

In every nook, a legend lies,
Unseen wonders beneath the skies.
From gnarled roots, old stories arise,
Fables inscribed in the world's disguise.

With every leaf that rustles soft,
Secrets of yore begin to waft.
Echoes of battles, of love and loss,
In this hidden realm, we bear the cross.

So let us wander, let us roam,
In fables found, we'll find our home.
Where whispered lore meets the realm divine,
The stories reveal what's truly mine.

Harmonies of the Unseen

In silence, blooms a symphony rare,
Harmonies linger in the cool night air.
The unseen world with rhythms to share,
Whispers and echoes dance everywhere.

With every heartbeat, a song is spun,
In shadows deep, where light is none.
Harmony flows in the space between,
In every breath, the unseen is keen.

Chords of the moonlight softly blend,
Melodies rise that never will end.
The unseen spirits in twilight sway,
Guiding our souls, showing the way.

Through the darkness, through joy and pain,
Harmonies weave, like a gentle rain.
In the fabric of night, our hearts align,
In the music of life, forever we shine.

Portals to the Beyond

Through shimmering gates, secrets sleep,
In twilight's embrace, dreams softly creep.
A whispering wind calls to the brave,
Step through the veil, the lost we save.

Ancient tales in starlit skies,
Hidden paths where wonder lies.
Casting echoes, the past unfolds,
A dance of magic, the heart beholds.

Crimson echoes of a time long past,
In visions bright, shadows are cast.
Open your heart, let the journey start,
For every portal reveals a new art.

In the silence, a world awaits,
Beyond the gates, enchanted fates.
Seek the light where shadows blend,
In realms of dusk, the magic transcends.

Enchanted Murmurs of Dusk

In the hush where shadows play,
The softest whispers come out to stay.
Beneath the boughs where secrets gleam,
Nighttime weaves a timeless dream.

Crickets sing their lullaby tune,
While fireflies dance 'neath the pale moon.
The air is thick with unseen charms,
Embracing each soul in gentle arms.

Echoes of laughter from distant lands,
Mysteries spun by invisible hands.
With every glance at the darkening sky,
We grasp for the stars, and let hopes fly.

In dusky hues, the world transforms,
Nature's magic in every form.
Hold tight the whispers, let spirits flow,
For in dusk's embrace, our wonders grow.

Whispers of Enchantment

In twilight's hush, soft secrets sigh,
The moonlight glimmers on fields nearby.
With every rustle, they stir and weave,
Tales of magic that none believe.

Candles flicker in the cool night air,
Ghostly figures dance without a care.
Echoes of laughter fill the night,
Drawn from shadows, embraced by light.

Each rustling leaf tells stories old,
Of love and valor, of hearts so bold.
In enchanted corners, dreams resound,
Hidden wonders waiting to be found.

Listen closely, the night calls near,
With whispers of enchantment ringing clear.
Embrace the magic, let your heart soar,
For in the stillness, there's so much more.

Shadows of the Wandering Sorcerer

In the twilight glow, shadows glide,
A sorcerer wanders, unseen, untried.
In cloak of night, with flickering spark,
He whispers spells that echo the dark.

Each step an echo through time untold,
Magic flows like silver and gold.
His eyes aglow with secrets profound,
In every corner, enchantment is found.

The moon bears witness to ancient arts,
As he weaves fate with masterful parts.
From deep within, the shadows arise,
Conjuring wonder beneath starlit skies.

With every whisper, the night does part,
Revealing the mysteries sweet and tart.
Follow the path where the shadows roam,
For the wandering sorcerer leads you home.

Serenade of the Enchanted Stream

Whispers of water dance and gleam,
Lulling the night with a gentle dream.
Moonbeams weave through the leafy shroud,
Nature's song rises, soft and loud.

Ripples carry secrets untold,
Stories of magic, daring and bold.
Silver fish dart beneath the flow,
In the enchanted current, time seems to slow.

Stars twinkle above, a watchful gaze,
Embraced by the night in a mysterious haze.
The stream sings on, forever it strives,
In its serenade, pure magic thrives.

So linger here, lost in the sound,
Where the heart of the forest quietly pounds.
Let the enchantment capture your soul,
As the serene waters endlessly roll.

Twilight's Spellbound Lament

Shadows gather as daylight wanes,
A sorrowful tune in the twilight reigns.
Colors blend in a soft embrace,
Fading light leaves a haunting trace.

Dusk whispers tales of joy and pain,
Stirring echoes that still remain.
In the stillness, memories swell,
Each heartbeat, a soft farewell.

The horizon bleeds with hues of despair,
A fragile moment, too pure to bear.
As stars ignite in their velvet sea,
Night wraps its arms around you and me.

In the dance of dark and light we find,
Secrets entwined, our fates aligned.
Through twilight's touch, we learn to yearn,
For in lament, our spirits burn.

The Unseen Threads of Fate

Invisible lines connect our souls,
Woven in patterns, the heart consoles.
A gentle tug, a whispering call,
Binding us close, lest we should fall.

In moments shared, a spark ignites,
Fate's silent dance, on starry nights.
The choices made, the paths we tread,
In every step, a story is fed.

Threads of destiny twine and weave,
In the fabric of life, we dream and believe.
Each twist and turn brings us to grace,
A tapestry bright, this wondrous place.

Though unseen forces may tug and sway,
Guiding our hearts along the way.
Through love and loss, we learn to create,
The intricate dance of our shared fate.

A Glimmering Veil of Wonder

Behind the curtain of the mundane,
Lies a realm of dreams, free from pain.
A glimmering veil, soft and bright,
Inviting us to explore its light.

Wonders awaken in twilight's embrace,
Magic unfurls, a timeless grace.
In whispered secrets, hope's soft sigh,
We find the courage to spread our wings and fly.

Colors of joy paint the vast sky,
Each stroke a promise, as we pass by.
With every heartbeat, the world comes alive,
In this veil of wonder, we truly thrive.

So take a moment, let your heart see,
The beauty around, in you and in me.
For in the glimmer, we're never alone,
Together in wonder, we've truly grown.

Reflections of Ancient Charms

In the stillness of the night,
Echoes of tales take flight,
Whispers of the ages past,
Charmed by shadows, ever cast.

Mysterious dances in the air,
Glimmers of dreams, soft and rare,
Each moment holds a fragrant hue,
Timeless tales woven anew.

Waves of stories gently rise,
In the depths, wisdom lies,
With every glance, a new delight,
Ancient whispers guide the night.

Beneath the stars, their glow remains,
Carved in time, in joy, in pains,
A tapestry of life unfolds,
Ancient charms, in silence, holds.

Twilight's Tapestry of Wonders

As day gives way to night's embrace,
A canvas stretches, soft in space,
Twilight paints the skies in gold,
Secrets of the day retold.

Stars awake in gentle sighs,
Moonbeams dance, a sweet reprise,
Whispers of the fading sun,
A symphony just begun.

Colors bleed, a wondrous sight,
Horizons blush in fading light,
Nature's brush, both bold and shy,
Marks the canvas of the sky.

In this moment, hearts align,
Lost in whispers, pure, divine,
Twilight's magic wraps us close,
In its glow, we feel the most.

Lurking Wonders Beneath the Surface

Beneath the waves, where silence reigns,
Lurking wonders bound by chains,
Secrets hide in depths unseen,
Mysteries wrapped in sea's cuisine.

Fins and tails in shades of blue,
Echoes of a world so true,
Coral castles, vibrant hues,
Guarding tales of ocean's muse.

In shadows cast by depths below,
Life thrives where few dare to go,
Ancient ruins, treasures laid,
In the quiet, dreams are made.

Bubbles rise from silent homes,
Whispers lost in liquid domes,
Every ripple holds a chance,
To explore the ocean's dance.

Lullabies of the Lost Realms

In the hush of twilight's grace,
Lies a world, a hidden place,
Whispers float on evening's breeze,
Sung by leaves upon the trees.

Forgotten echoes call the night,
Melodies of lost delight,
Haunting dreams wrapped in a sigh,
Lullabies that never die.

Through the mists of ages past,
Stories linger, shadows cast,
Carried on the winds so light,
Secrets woven in the night.

Close your eyes and drift away,
To the realms where lost things play,
In every note, a tale so deep,
Lullabies that softly sweep.

Phantoms of Enchanted Revelations

In twilight's glow, whispers entwine,
Shadows dance, secrets divine.
Echoes of laughter float on the air,
Beneath the stars, lost souls declare.

With flickering lights, they weave their tales,
Through ancient woods, where silence prevails.
Phantoms in gowns of gleaming white,
Guide the dreamers through the night.

Their eyes hold stories of loves long past,
Fleeting moments that forever last.
In this realm where time stands still,
Magic lingers, a haunting thrill.

So listen close to the evening's song,
With phantom hearts, we all belong.
In every sigh and gentle breeze,
Revelations bloom among the trees.

The Alchemy of Dreams and Shadows

In the cauldron of night, secrets churn,
Dreams are crafted, and shadows burn.
Whispers of fate dance in the dark,
While starlit echoes leave their mark.

A potion of hope, a tincture of fear,
Brewing the visions we hold dear.
With every breath, magic ignites,
Transforming silence into delights.

Waves of wonder crash on the shore,
Infinite dreams, always seeking more.
Underneath the veil, mysteries glow,
The alchemy of hearts, a gentle flow.

So close your eyes, let visions stream,
In the depths of night, you'll find your dream.
And when dawn breaks, let shadows dance,
For life is but a fleeting chance.

Traces of Spells in the Stardust

In the night sky, where stardust drifts,
Whispers of magic, cosmic gifts.
Each twinkle writes a story untold,
In the tapestry of the brave and bold.

From ancient spells, the cosmos sings,
Of love and loss, of fleeting things.
With every star, a wish takes flight,
In the celestial quilt, pure and bright.

Fingers trace the paths above,
Reminders of dreams and the power of love.
Through the vast expanse, we seek our place,
In the nebula's embrace, we find grace.

So gather the stardust, hold it tight,
A sprinkle of magic to guide the night.
In every shimmer, feel the glow,
For traces of spells will help you know.

Starbound Chronicles of Wonder

Beyond the horizon, where dreams unfold,
   Starbound journeys, stories untold.
 In the tapestry woven by cosmic hands,
   Adventures await in distant lands.

With each shooting star, wishes ignite,
Chasing the shadows, seeking the light.
  Timeless tales in the celestial air,
  Carried on winds, a kindred flare.

In the galaxy's heart, mysteries bloom,
Each moment echoes in the quiet room.
Hearts aflame with the spirit of roam,
 In the starlit night, we find our home.

So journey forth, let your spirit soar,
For every star holds a dream to explore.
In the chronicles of wonder, we partake,
  Bound by the light, we dare to wake.

Threads of Celestial Wonder

In the night sky, stars weave tales,
Of ancient dreams and cosmic trails.
Galaxies spin in a silent song,
Binding space where we all belong.

The moon whispers secrets of old,
Casting silver on streets so bold.
Planets dance in harmonious sway,
Painting night into the day.

Nebulas glow in colors bright,
Embracing the fabric of twilight.
Every twinkle, a life once shared,
A connection in darkness, declared.

So we gaze and ponder the skies,
Chasing wonders beyond our eyes.
In each shimmer, our hopes align,
Threads of wonder, eternally twine.

The Dance of Fading Lights

In dusk's embrace, shadows arise,
Fading lights kiss the skies.
Crickets sing their evening tune,
As stars awaken, one by one.

The horizon swallows the sun's glow,
Painting the night in hues of woe.
Each flicker, a story untold,
Mysteries wrapped in silken folds.

Whispers of darkness start to sway,
Cascading dreams that drift away.
In twilight's arms, we find our flight,
Navigating through the cloak of night.

Yet within the shadows and fright,
Still shines the essence of light.
A dance of fading, a gentle fall,
Love and hope bind it all.

Riddles of the Whispering Winds

Through rustling leaves, a secret breathes,
Carried on winds, like wandering thieves.
They speak of stories, old and wise,
In every gust, a new disguise.

Whispers echo in fields of gold,
Revealing mysteries yet untold.
A playful breeze, it swirls about,
Chasing thoughts, erasing doubt.

The wind, a bard of nature's song,
Guiding hearts where they belong.
With every sigh, a chance to learn,
In its embrace, lost souls return.

So listen closely to its call,
In the silence, you won't fall.
For in the dance of whispered lore,
The winds unravel forevermore.

Shimmering Glimmers of Time

Time flows like a river, so bright,
With glimmers of moments, pure delight.
In fleeting glances, memories shine,
A tapestry woven, forever entwined.

Each second whispers, a fleeting grace,
Marks of laughter on time's soft face.
As hours twirl like leaves in flight,
Creating magic in day and night.

Glimmers fading, yet still they glow,
In the depths of our hearts, they know.
The past holds treasures, love's gentle chime,
A reminder: we're lost in time.

So hold each moment, let it shine,
In shimmering glimmers, divine.
For life is a dance, vibrant and free,
A symphony played for you and me.

Revelations in Secret Sylvan Gardens

In shadows deep where secrets grow,
The whispers of the trees do flow.
A dance of light through leaves entwined,
In silent beauty, truths we find.

Each petal soft, a tale unfolds,
Of ancient dreams and visions bold.
The moonlit paths invite the hearts,
Where nature's song in stillness starts.

Beneath the arch of emerald boughs,
The past and present take their vows.
Each rustling leaf a story shared,
In sylvan realms, we are laid bare.

In gardens where the spirits play,
We wander lost in the ballet.
With every breath, a secret blooms,
In quiet nodes, the magic looms.

The Clockwork of Fantastical Journeys

Ticking gears beneath the skies,
A world of wonder in disguise.
With every turn, the dreams arise,
In clockwork realms where magic lies.

A compass spins with tales untold,
Through realms of silver, blue, and gold.
Each second ticks a path anew,
As travels beckon me and you.

Through portals wide, we leap and glide,
With every chime, the worlds collide.
In time's embrace, adventures bloom,
Within the clockwork's rhythmic tune.

The hands of fate guide every pulse,
In fantasy, the heart convulse.
With whispers soft, the journeys call,
In realms of time, we rise and fall.

Ethereal Bridges Across Dimensions

Across the void, where shadows play,
Ethereal bridges lead the way.
They shimmer bright in the starlit night,
Connecting worlds with beams of light.

Each step we take upon this path,
Unveils the echoes of the past.
In realms where time and space align,
Our souls entwined in design divine.

With whispers soft where dreams reside,
We gather secrets side by side.
In every blink, new vistas rise,
Eternal truths beneath the skies.

These bridges span the great unknown,
In every leap, our spirits grown.
Through cosmic dance, we find our place,
In dimensions rich with warm embrace.

Fables Danced on the Breezes

In twilight's glow, the fables weave,
On whispers soft, we dare believe.
Each story borne on gentle air,
A tapestry of dreams laid bare.

The breezes carry tales of old,
Of kingdoms lost and heroes bold.
In every gust, a voice we hear,
The laughter, love, the masked fear.

With every rustle in the trees,
A fable stirs, ignites the breeze.
From ancient lore, to modern plight,
In every breath, the stories light.

So let the winds of fable sing,
And guide our hopes on airy wing.
In gentle breezes, magic sways,
As we embrace the dance of days.

Whispers of Enchantment

In the forest deep and dark,
Where secrets softly spark,
Fairy lights dance through the trees,
Carried gently by the breeze.

Echoes of ancient tales unfold,
In the warmth of dusk, bold.
Magic lingers in the air,
Whispers cradle every prayer.

Each petal glows with a dream,
Silently weaving their seam,
Underneath the silver moon,
A symphony begins to croon.

In this realm where shadows play,
Hold your heart and drift away,
For enchanted nights do keep,
The wondrous hopes that we seek.

Dreams Beneath Starlit Skies

Beneath the vast and twinkling dome,
Where silver stars sweetly roam,
Whispers float on midnight air,
Cradling dreams beyond compare.

Each wish, a spark of cosmic grace,
Dances gently in this space,
As constellations start to sing,
Of mysteries that night can bring.

In the quiet, hearts align,
With every sip of moonlit wine,
Together we weave a tapestry,
Of dreams entwined in harmony.

So close your eyes and take flight,
In the dark, find your light,
For beneath the starlit skies,
Your hopes shall rise, your spirit flies.

The Alchemist's Lullaby

In a chamber filled with glass,
Where secrets of the night amass,
A gentle hum begins to rise,
The alchemist's soft lullabies.

With potions brewed from ancient lore,
Each note unlocks an unseen door,
Through shadows deep, the journey flows,
A path where only wisdom grows.

The starlit spark in every vial,
Transforms the bleak with a golden smile,
As dreams are mixed with whispered charms,
Casting spells with open arms.

So let the night enfold your heart,
In magic's realm, we play our part,
For every sigh and tranquil sigh,
Brims the world with alchemist's cry.

Shadows of Forgotten Spells

In the corners where dust congregates,
Rest the shadows that time abates,
Echoes of spells once deeply cast,
Whispers of magic lost to the past.

Beneath the weight of ancient tomes,
Lies a world where darkness roams,
Faint glimmers of power reside,
Waiting for hearts that confide.

Through tangled roots and silent stones,
Reverberate familiar tones,
Calling forth dreams repressed,
In the stillness, shadows rest.

So seek the light behind the gray,
Let the past guide your way,
For in those shadows, sparks implore,
The magic that lies at your door.

Whispers of the Timeless Enigma

In shadows cast by ancient trees,
A secret lingers on the breeze.
The echoes of forgotten lore,
Whispered soft, forevermore.

With every breath, the ages sigh,
As stars above begin to fly.
Time's embrace, a fragile thread,
In twilight dreams, the past is fed.

A puzzle carved in silence deep,
Awakens thoughts that gently creep.
Unlock the doors within your mind,
Where truth and mystery entwined.

The night unfolds its mystic tale,
With shadows dancing, soft and pale.
An enigma wrapped in night's embrace,
Whispers of time, a sacred space.

Guardians of the Enchanted Realm

In the heart of woods so deep,
Ancient beings wake from sleep.
Guardians of the hidden glades,
Where magic blooms and never fades.

Through tangled vines and silver streams,
They protect the world of dreams.
With eyes that shine like morning dew,
Their watchful gaze is always true.

In each rustle, a story unfolds,
Of forgotten myths and whispered golds.
The trees stand tall, their secrets bared,
In this realm, all hearts are shared.

Dancing leaves tell tales of old,
Where bravery and love are bold.
The guardians raise their voices high,
In harmony with earth and sky.

Silhouettes in the Moonlit Grove

Beneath the moon's soft, silver glow,
Silhouettes in shadows flow.
Figures dance with gentle grace,
In the grove, a sacred place.

Whispers echo through the night,
Stars above, a guiding light.
With each step, a story told,
In the silence, dreams unfold.

The breeze carries a sweet refrain,
In the heart, a subtle pain.
For every love that was once true,
Leaves a trace beneath the blue.

As nightingale sings soft and low,
The silhouettes begin to flow.
A tapestry of light and dark,
In the grove, we leave our mark.

The Riddle of the Mystic Winds

The winds whisper secrets, old and wise,
Carrying tales from distant skies.
Through valleys deep and mountains high,
Echoes of time that never die.

Each gust a riddle, softly spun,
A dance of shadows in the sun.
With laughter, they sweep the earth,
Breathing life into dreams of birth.

In quiet moments, listen close,
For nature sings, and hearts do boast.
The winds weave through the trees so grand,
With riddles held in their gentle hand.

As daylight fades and dusk descends,
The mystic winds, they twist and bend.
Unraveling truths in twilight's kiss,
A world unknown awaits in bliss.

The Charm of Forgotten Lullabies

In whispers soft, the shadows play,
A melody from yesterday.
The cradle rocks, the world stands still,
As twilight weaves its gentle will.

Songs of stars in the evening glow,
Echoes sweet that ebb and flow.
Memory's breath on a moonlit night,
Cradled dreams take graceful flight.

Voices lost in the misty haze,
Lullabies of forgotten days.
Each note a sigh, a love reborn,
In the quiet, a heart is worn.

So hush your doubts, let slumber reign,
Embrace the past, release the pain.
For in these songs, the heart will find,
The charm of peace, forever kind.

Echos Beneath the Surface of Time

Beneath the surface, whispers dwell,
Stories untold, secrets to tell.
The river flows, a timeless stream,
Reflecting shadows of a dream.

Moments linger in the silent air,
Echoes of laughter, traces of care.
Fleeting glimpses, a fleeting sigh,
Caught in the web where memories lie.

Time's embrace, a delicate thread,
Weaving paths where we once tread.
In depths unknown, the heart will soar,
Past the known, to seek once more.

So listen close with an open heart,
For in the echoes, we find a start.
A journey marked by love's own rhyme,
Lost and found, beneath time's climb.

The Portrait of a Dreamweaver

With colors bright and shadows deep,
A tapestry of dreams to keep.
In quiet strokes, the canvas glows,
A world where imagination flows.

Faces dance in whispers bold,
Stories spun from threads of gold.
Each brush a wish, a timeless flight,
In the portrait of the starry night.

Eyes that see beyond the veil,
Whispers of hope in every tale.
Each scene a spark, a fleeting grace,
Captured moments, in time's embrace.

So let the weaver spin away,
Through dreams and colors, night and day.
For in each stroke, a piece of soul,
The portrait lives, forever whole.

Enigmas of the Wandering Night

In shadows cast, the mysteries wait,
Wandering souls at a silent gate.
The moon a guide in the darkened sky,
Whispers float as stars drift by.

Veils of midnight, secrets confide,
A journey taken through paths untried.
Each footstep soft, in twilight's grace,
Unraveling tales in this hidden space.

Chasing echoes of forgotten dreams,
Lost in the glow of silver beams.
The night unfolds its tender charms,
Wrapping hearts in its endless arms.

So wander forth, embrace the dark,
For in the shadows, you'll find your spark.
Each enigma a key, unlocking the light,
In the magic of the wandering night.

The Dance of the Ethereal Spirits

In twilight glows the spirits sway,
With whispers soft, they find their way.
Veils of mist in moonlight weave,
A sacred dance the night believe.

They twirl and spin in timeless grace,
A tapestry of cosmic space.
Each flicker bright, a tale untold,
In shadows deep, their secrets hold.

Around the stones where shadows play,
Ancient echoes call and stay.
The forest breathes, it's come alive,
In harmony, the spirits thrive.

As dawn approaches, fading light,
The spirits bow and take to flight.
Yet in our hearts, they leave their trace,
A gentle kiss, a soft embrace.

Fables from the Edge of Reality

In realms where dreams and truth collide,
Fables flourish, fears subside.
A whisper heard, a shadow cast,
Stories woven, futures vast.

Beneath the stars, the ancients speak,
Of journeys long, of hearts that seek.
Through twisting paths, the lost will roam,
Chasing echoes that guide them home.

Each tale a thread of twisted fate,
In the silence, we contemplate.
What lurks beyond the world we see?
The edge holds truths we long to be.

With every fable, wisdom grows,
In haunted woods, the river flows.
The breath of ghosts ignites the night,
These edges shimmer, pure delight.

The Lure of Phantasmal Dreams

In slumber deep, the visions rise,
Phantasmal sights, a sweet surprise.
Where starlit waters softly gleam,
Awakening the heart's own dream.

Across the void, the voices call,
Chasing dreams that softly fall.
A mosaic of hopes and fears,
In every laugh reside the tears.

Each journey brings a fleeting glance,
A wisp of magic, a fleeting chance.
Threads of dreams in twilight spun,
A chase of shadows just begun.

In spectral realms where wonders gleam,
We tread the path of endless dream.
With every breath, we delve anew,
In phantasmal realms where wishes brew.

Luminescent Secrets in the Night

Beneath the stars, a glow unfolds,
Luminescent secrets, softly told.
The night reveals its hidden lore,
As whispered tides rush to the shore.

Moonlight dances on emerald leaves,
In the stillness, the heart believes.
Each spark of light, a story shines,
In the quiet, the universe aligns.

From ancient trees to shimmering streams,
The night is rich with woven dreams.
With every flicker, shadows blend,
Bringing whispers from the stars to mend.

In the darkness, wonder wakes,
As softly like the dawn, it breaks.
Those luminescent secrets speak,
A gentle truth that all hearts seek.

Ballad of the Starlit Traveler

Under a sky where the stars gleam bright,
A wanderer roams through the cool, soft night.
With whispers of secrets the heavens share,
He follows their trail with a heart laid bare.

Across the valleys, over the hills,
Every breath taken, the night time thrills.
The moon guides his steps with a silver glow,
While dreams of adventure within him grow.

With each gentle breeze that caresses his skin,
He finds hidden paths where the journey can begin.
The starlight dances like fireflies' flight,
Illuminating hopes in the velvet night.

So onward he ventures, never to tire,
A traveler bound by the songs of desire.
With the cosmos above and his spirit so free,
In the ballad of night, he finds his decree.

Captured Moments of the Arcane

In shadows deep where whispers reside,
A sorcerer spins with secrets to hide.
With gestures subtle, he crafts his art,
Captured moments that dance from the heart.

The flicker of candles, a spark in the night,
Each spell woven softly, a delicate sight.
The air thick with magic, a promise untold,
Stories of ages in the dust of old.

Each potion a picture, a glance through the veil,
Be it sorrow or joy, each story won't fail.
In the cauldron's swirl, memories align,
Symbolic and fleeting, like sunlight that shines.

Thus journey the threads of what once was and is,
In the realm of the arcane, there's always a whiz.
Through shadows and laughter, with grace they combine,
In captured moments, eternity shines.

Flames of a Forgotten Alchemist

In a dim-lit chamber, where secrets unfold,
An alchemist whispers of treasures untold.
With beakers and flasks that bubble and brew,
He seeks out the whispers of what once he knew.

The flames dance lightly, a flickering trace,
Illuminating the dreams hidden in space.
Each formula scribed, a tale of the past,
Of knowledge once cherished that faded too fast.

He toils through the night, the nightingale sings,
As the echoes of history on warm hearths take wings.
With patience and flame, he conjures the night,
Invoking the shadows, igniting the light.

Yet as embers fade, so too does his quest,
For the flames of remembrance may never find rest.
In the heart of the dark, the alchemist lies,
A guardian of secrets, beneath ancient skies.

The Muse of Celestial Night

Beneath the stars, she twirls with grace,
The muse of night, in her cosmic space.
With whispers of wonder, she breaks the dawn,
In blankets of starlight, dreams are drawn.

Her laughter cascades like a river of light,
Guiding the lost through the depths of the night.
Each heartbeat resonates with galactic tune,
As shadows transform into wonders that swoon.

She weaves through the silence, a song in the air,
In realms of the dreamers, she lingers with care.
Her presence ignites inspiration's spark,
Like fireflies dancing in the velvety dark.

So, sing to the muse who dwells in the skies,
With stars as her jewels and hope in her eyes.
Embrace the celestial, let your spirit soar,
For in her kind solace, we yearn for no more.

Harmonics of the Heart's Desire

In whispers soft, our secrets play,
They dance on chords of night and day.
Each note unfolds, a tender sigh,
Resonance found where dreams can fly.

With every beat, the shadows fade,
In twilight's glow, our hearts parade.
A melody that draws us near,
Together we break every fear.

In passion's tune, we find our way,
Across the vast and starry sway.
The music swells, in perfect rhyme,
Eternal echoes, lost in time.

Embrace the sound, let it entwine,
Two souls as one, forever shine.
The harmonics of our heart's tune,
A symphony beneath the moon.

Fantasies Born of Myth

In ancient woods where shadows creep,
Legends wake from their eternal sleep.
With woven tales, the stars align,
In dreams of old, the truths combine.

A dragon's roar, a whispering breeze,
Fables told beneath the trees.
Heroes rise from ashes cold,
Their stories carved in hearts of gold.

Elixirs poured from goblet bright,
Magic flows through the endless night.
Wonders bloom where hope persists,
Fantasies born in twilight mists.

So close your eyes and take the flight,
Through realms of wonder, pure delight.
In myth and dream, we'll find our place,
Together dwell in timeless grace.

The Song of the Wandering Sage

Through valleys deep and mountains high,
A wandering sage, beneath the sky.
With every step, the tales unfold,
Of wisdom rich, and spirits bold.

He sings of lands where wildflowers bloom,
And dances lightly through the gloom.
The echoes of his voice resound,
In every heart, the truth is found.

With a gentle smile and knowing gaze,
He shares the light of endless days.
A journey vast, a spirit free,
His song connects both you and me.

So heed his words and roam afar,
For in your soul, you are the star.
The song of life in every page,
Resonates with the wandering sage.

Threads of Time and Twilight

In twilight's grasp, the moments weave,
Threads of time, in layers, believe.
Each strand a story, soft yet bright,
Entwined in echoes of fading light.

The clock ticks slow, yet swiftly flies,
In dreams of dusk, where silence lies.
Each moment holds a precious grace,
A tapestry of time and place.

With every heartbeat, shadows blend,
As yesterday meets the virtues penned.
The past and future, hand in hand,
We sketch our fate upon this land.

So cherish now, this gift we share,
For threads of time are rare and fair.
In twilight's glow, we find our way,
A dance of souls at end of day.

The Allure of Celestial Mysteries

In the night sky, stars gleam bright,
Whispers of worlds far from our sight.
Galaxies turning, a cosmic dance,
Inviting the dreamer to take a chance.

Veils of darkness cloak the unknown,
Curiosity seeds are easily sown.
Planets align in a shimmering row,
Echoing stories of ages ago.

Comets blaze trails, a fleeting sight,
Guiding us through the velvet night.
Each twinkle shines with a hidden song,
A melody sweet where we all belong.

Cradled in dreams of immortal stars,
Hope resides beneath Jupiter's scars.
The allure of mysteries, vast and grand,
Awakens the wanderer's yearning hand.

Dreams Woven in Starlight

In slumber's embrace, the starlight glows,
Weaving together the dreams we chose.
Whispers of futures that still remain,
Dancing through shadows like soft, sweet rain.

Between the stars, our wishes entwine,
Threads of our fates in the night align.
With each heartbeat, our spirits soar,
Into the cosmos, forevermore.

Luminous trails guide our restless hearts,
Mapping a journey where magic starts.
In every twinkle, a promise lies,
A glimpse of the truth that never dies.

So let the starlight cradle your fears,
In the tapestry woven through all of the years.
For in dreams, we find what we seek,
A universe vast, where souls can speak.

Secrets Beneath the Silver Moon

The silver moon graces the tranquil night,
Casting soft shadows in gentle light.
Secrets unfurl where the wild winds blow,
Echoing tales the ancients know.

Whispers of love painted in the skies,
Cradled in silence, where mystery lies.
Each glance of the moon, a story unfolds,
In its serene glow, the universe holds.

Under its gaze, the world feels new,
A dance of delights, hidden from view.
In the quiet moments, truths intertwine,
Revealing the magic in life's design.

With every cycle, it beckons us near,
To find the enchantments we hold dear.
Secrets beneath the silver moonlight,
Guide us through darkness and into the bright.

The Conductor of Hidden Realms

In shadows deep, where whispers play,
A conductor calls, guiding the way.
With a flick of a wrist, the worlds unfold,
Revealing wonders, both timid and bold.

Each note he strikes echoes through the night,
Awakening visions hidden from sight.
The fabric of dreams, a delicate thread,
Stitched by the hands where the mystics tread.

Through intricate patterns, he dances along,
Tuning the heartstrings to a timeless song.
In the symphony of life, we all take part,
Conducted by whispers that linger in heart.

So listen intently to the music's call,
A journey awaits, inviting us all.
The conductor of realms, in shadows he stands,
Leading us forth with his magical hands.

Milton Keynes UK
Ingram Content Group UK Ltd.
UKHW022144111124
451073UK00007B/190

9 789916 900840